KIDS' TRAVEL GUIDE

NEW YORK CITY

FlyingKids Presents:

KIDS' TRAVEL GUIDE
NEW YORK CITY

Author: Kelsey Fox, Shiela H. Leon

Editor: Carma Graber

Designer: Slavisa Zivkovic

Cover design: Francesca Guido

Illustrations: Slavisa Zivkovic, Francesca Guido

Published by FlyingKids

Visit us @ www.theflyingkids.com

Contact us: leonardo@theflyingkids.com

ISBN 978-1508459859

This is the only page for parents in this book ...

Dear Parents,

If you bought this book, you're probably planning a family trip with your kids. You are spending a lot of time and money in the hopes that this family vacation will be pleasant and fun. Of course, you would like your children to get to know the city you are visiting—a little of its geography, local history, **important sites**, culture, customs, and more. And you hope they will always remember the trip as a very special experience.

The reality is often quite different. Parents find themselves frustrated as they struggle to convince their kids to join a tour or visit a landmark, while the kids just want to stay in and watch TV. Or the kids are glued to their mobile devices and don't pay much attention to the new sights and places of interest. Many parents are disappointed when they return home and discover that their **kids don't remember** much about the trip and the new things they learned. That's exactly why the Kids' Travel Guide series was created.

With the Kids' Travel Guides, young children become researchers and active participants in the trip. During the vacation, kids will read relevant facts about the city you are visiting. The Kids' Travel Guides include puzzles, tasks to complete, useful tips, and other recommendations along the way. The kids will meet Leonardo—their tour guide. Leonardo encourages them to experiment, explore, and be more **involved in the family's activities**—as well as to learn new information and make memories throughout the trip. In addition, kids are encouraged to document and write about their experiences during the trip, so that when you return home, they will have a memoir that will be fun to look at and reread again and again.

The Kids' Travel Guides support children as they **get ready** for the trip, visit new places, learn new things, and finally, return **home**.

The ***Kids' Travel Guide — New York City*** focuses on The Big Apple. In it, children will find background information on New York City and its special attractions. The ***Kids' Travel Guide — New York City*** concentrates on central sites that are recommended for children. At each of these sites, interesting facts, action items, and quizzes await your kids.

You, the parents, are invited to participate or to find an available bench and relax while you enjoy your active children. If you are traveling to New York City, you may also want to get the *Kids' Travel Guide — USA*. It focuses on the country of the United States—its geography, history, unique culture, traditions, and more—using the fun and interesting style of the Kids' Travel Guide series.

Have a great Family Trip!

Hi, Kids !

Seals of New York City (left) and
New York State (right)

If you are reading this book, it means you are lucky—you are going to New York City!

You may have noticed that your parents are getting ready for the journey. They have bought travel guides, looked for information on the Internet, and printed pages of information. They are talking to friends and people who have already visited New York City, in order to learn about it and know what to do, where to go, and when ... But this is not just another guidebook for your parents.

This book is for you only—the young traveler.

So what is this book all about?

First and foremost, meet Leonardo, your very own personal guide on this trip. Leonardo has visited many places around the world. (Guess how he got there?) He will be with you throughout the book and the trip. Leonardo will tell you all about the places you will visit ... It is always good to learn a little about the city you are visiting and its history beforehand. Leonardo will give you many ideas, quizzes, tips, and other surprises. He will accompany you while you are packing and leaving home. He will stay in the hotel with you (don't worry—it doesn't cost more money)! And he will see the sights with you until you return home.

Have Fun!

A travel Diary—the beginning!
GOING TO NEW YORK CITY !!!

How did you get to New York?

By plane ✈ / train 🚆 / car 🚗 / other _____

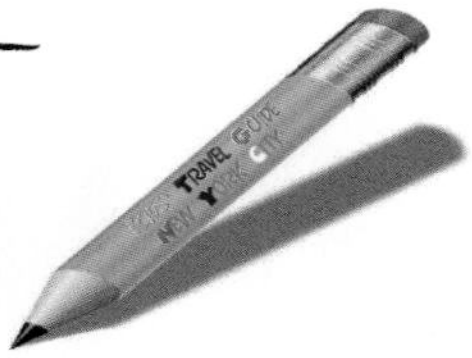

Date of arrival _____   Time _____

Date of departure _____

All in all, we will stay in New York City for _____ days.

Is this your first visit?   **YES**   **NO**

Where will you sleep?
In a hotel / in an apartment / with friends or family / other _____

What sites are you planning to visit?

_____

_____

_____

What special activities are you planning to do?

_____

_____

Are you excited about the trip?

This is an excitement indicator. Ask your family members how excited they are (from "not at all" up to "very, very much"), and mark each of their answers on the indicator. Leonardo has already marked the level of his excitement ...

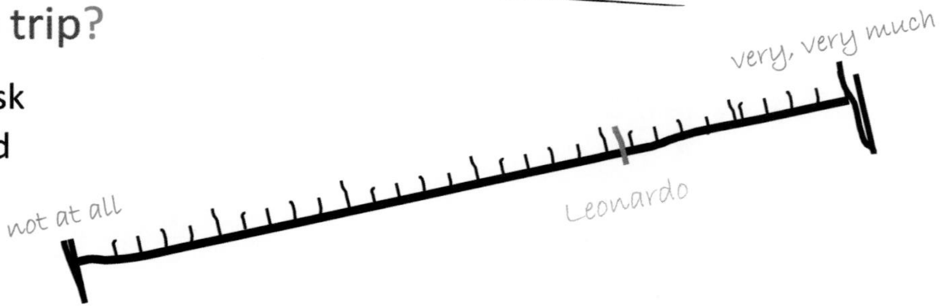

very, very much

Leonardo

not at all

Who is traveling?

Write down the names of the family members traveling with you and their answers to the questions.

PASTE A PICTURE OF YOUR FAMILY.

Name: _____

Age: _____

Has he or she visited **New York City** before? yes / no

WHAT IS THE MOST EXCITING
THING ABOUT YOUR UPCOMING TRIP?

_____
_____

Name: _____

Age: _____

Has he or she visited **New York City** before? yes / no

WHAT IS THE MOST EXCITING
THING ABOUT YOUR UPCOMING TRIP?

_____
_____

Name: _____

Age: _____

Has he or she visited **New York City** before? yes / no

WHAT IS THE MOST EXCITING
THING ABOUT YOUR UPCOMING TRIP?

_____
_____

Name: _____

Age: _____

Has he or she visited **New York City** before? yes / no

WHAT IS THE MOST EXCITING
THING ABOUT YOUR UPCOMING TRIP?

_____
_____

Name: _____

Age: _____

Has he or she visited **New York City** before? yes / no

WHAT IS THE MOST EXCITING
THING ABOUT YOUR UPCOMING TRIP?

_____
_____

Preparations at home –
DO NOT FORGET ....!

Mom or Dad will take care of packing clothes (how many pairs of pants, which comb to take ...). So Leonardo will only tell you about the stuff he thinks you may want to bring along to New York City.

Here's the Packing List Leonardo made for you. You can check off each item as you pack it:

- *Kids' Travel Guide — New York City*—of course!
- Comfortable walking shoes
- A raincoat (One that folds up is best—sometimes it rains without warning ...)
- A hat (and sunglasses, if you want)
- Pens and pencils
- Crayons and markers (It is always nice to color and paint.)
- A notebook or writing pad (You can use it for games or writing, or to draw or doodle in when you're bored ...)
- A book to read
- Your smartphone/tablet or camera
- _____
- _____

Pack your things in a small bag (or backpack). You may also want to take these things:

Snacks, fruit, candy, and chewing gum. If you are flying, it can help a lot during takeoff and landing, when there's pressure in your ears 😮.

Some games you can play while sitting down: electronic games, booklets of crossword puzzles, connect-the-numbers, etc.

Now let's see if you can find 12 items you should take on a trip in this word search puzzle:

- [ ] Leonardo
- [ ] walking shoes
- [ ] hat
- [ ] raincoat
- [ ] crayons
- [x] book
- [ ] pencil
- [ ] camera
- [ ] snacks
- [ ] fruit
- [ ] patience
- [ ] good mood

P	A	T	I	E	N	C	E	A	W	F	G
E	L	R	T	S	G	Y	J	W	A	T	O
Q	E	Y	U	Y	K	Z	K	M	L	W	O
H	O	S	N	A	S	N	Y	S	K	G	D
A	N	R	Z	C	P	E	N	C	I	L	M
C	A	M	E	R	A	A	W	G	N	E	O
R	R	A	I	N	C	O	A	T	G	Q	O
Y	D	S	G	I	R	K	Z	K	S	H	D
S	O	A	C	O	A	E	T	K	H	A	T
F	R	U	I	T	Y	Q	O	V	O	D	A
B	O	O	K	F	O	H	Z	K	E	R	T
T	K	Z	K	A	N	S	I	E	S	Y	U
O	V	I	E	S	S	N	A	C	K	S	P

New York, New York!

New York City is a huge city in the state of New York.

New York State sits on the northeast coast of the United States of America. It is bordered by the states of New Jersey and Pennsylvania to the south, and the states of Connecticut, Massachusetts, and Vermont to the east. New York also shares an international border with Canada.

Can you help Leonardo find all New York's neighbor states? _____

Twenty-six states are bigger than New York in size, but New York is third in number of people. Only California and Texas have more people than New York.

Quizzes!

Name three states that are bigger in size than New York. *Look at the map if you need help.*

ANSWERS

There are many states bigger than New York. Here are some of them: Alaska, Texas, California, Montana, New Mexico, Arizona, Nevada.

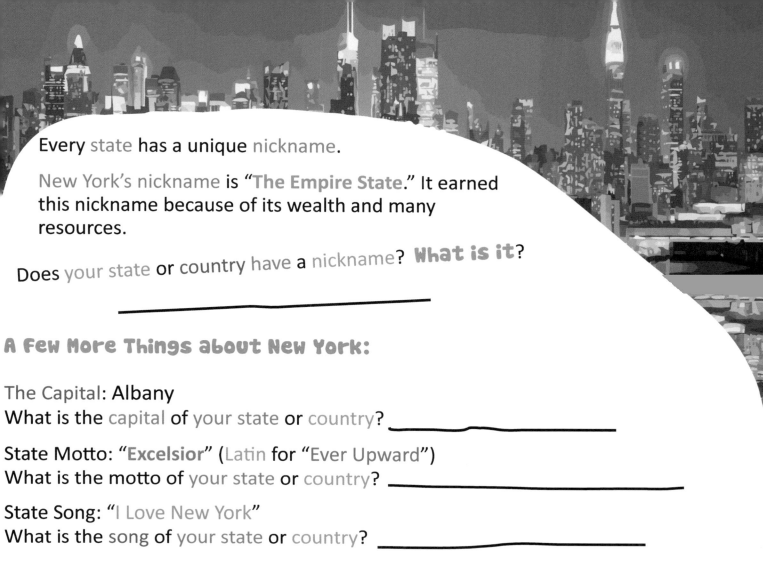

Every state has a unique nickname.

New York's nickname is "**The Empire State**." It earned this nickname because of its wealth and many resources.

Does your state or country have a nickname? **What is it**?

_____

A Few More Things about New York:

The Capital: **Albany**
What is the capital of your state or country? _____

State Motto: "**Excelsior**" (Latin for "Ever Upward")
What is the motto of your state or country? _____

State Song: "I Love New York"
What is the song of your state or country? _____

New York City, Here We Come!

In size, New York City is actually a very small part of New York State. But more than 40 percent of the people in the state live in New York City 😮!

Much of the city is on an island called **Manhattan**. New York City is known for its great entertainment, world-famous museums, special buildings and stores, and its many historical sites. It is a popular spot for families to visit because there are so many fun things to do and see.

New York City is especially enjoyable if you love to eat! It's often called "America's Melting Pot," because so many people from different parts of the world come to live in the city. They bring their country's foods and customs with them. Many of them have even opened restaurants to share their food with others. During your trip to New York, pay special attention to all the different types of foods you see and eat.

11

What does New York City look like?

When we say "New York City," we really mean the five neighborhoods, called boroughs, that make up the much larger city. The five boroughs are Brooklyn, Bronx, Manhattan, Queens, and Staten Island. You can visit a place in any of these boroughs, and you will still be in New York City.

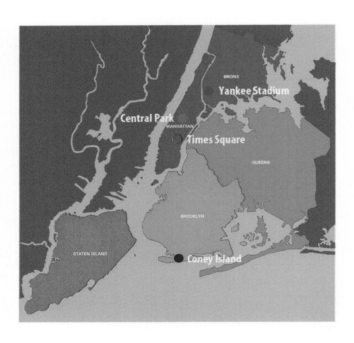

In Which Boroughs Are These Sites Located?

Yankee Stadium
_____

Central Park
_____

Coney Island
_____

Times Square
_____

Where I'm staying
_____

Did you know?
New York City is also known as "The Big Apple," "The City That Never Sleeps," "New Amsterdam," and "The Melting Pot." Can you think why **NYC** earned these nicknames?

ANSWERS
Yankee Stadium is in the Bronx; Central Park is in Manhattan; Coney Island is in Brooklyn; Times Square is in Manhattan.

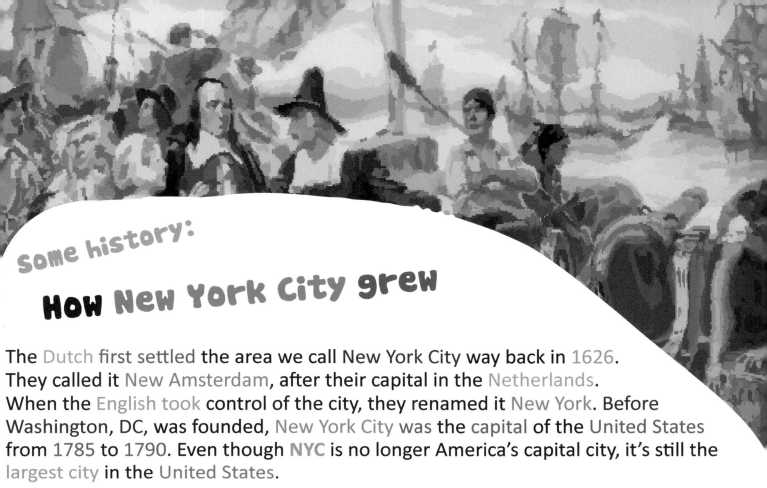

Some history:

How New York City grew

The Dutch first settled the area we call New York City way back in 1626. They called it New Amsterdam, after their capital in the Netherlands. When the English took control of the city, they renamed it New York. Before Washington, DC, was founded, New York City was the capital of the United States from 1785 to 1790. Even though **NYC** is no longer America's capital city, it's still the largest city in the United States.

New York has become one of the most important cities in the world. It is well-known for theater, art, finance, politics, and business. It is the home of Broadway, Wall Street, the United Nations building, famous museums, and many powerful companies.

The city has many opportunities to offer. That is one of the reasons thousands of people traveled here from other countries to start a new life. Ellis Island and the Statue of Liberty became symbols of hope and fortune to those seeking a better life in America.

Did you know?
New York City's Police Department—called the **NYPD**—is the largest police department in the United States. They have over 35,000 sworn officers. The **NYPD** has a long and proud history of fighting mobsters and other organized crime 😮.

Getting around NYC

There are many exciting ways to get around in **NYC** that may be different from how you travel at home. Check the box for every kind of transportation you tried while visiting!

☐ Walking

Many people walk around, hurrying from one place to the next. Walking is a great way to people watch. Look at all the different kinds of people there are in this one place!

☐ Taxi

Yellow taxicabs have become a famous way of traveling around the city. Cab drivers must buy a medallion to put on their cars. The medallion can cost over $700,000. That would be enough to buy your parents about 23 cars! Cab drivers are not allowed to operate a cab in **NYC** without one of these medallions. *How many medallions can you spot* 😊 ? _____

☐ Subway

The **NYC** subway is a train system that spreads out all over the city. Most of the subway trains travel underground. It is one of the biggest and oldest public transportation systems in the world.

Only in NYC

☐ **Dylan's Candy Bar**

Dylan's Candy Bar is the world's largest candy store! They have unusual treats like candy tape and gummy animals.

☐ **Children's Museum of Manhattan**

Visit Snoopy and other pals in this museum that's especially for kids.

☐ **Grand Central Terminal**

This train station is one of the largest and most beautiful in the world. It's also known as Grand Central Station.

☐ **Chinatown**

Here you'll find Chinese customs and foods, and discover the history of the Chinese in America.

Central Park—
outdoor fun in the City

Central Park is a large park located in Manhattan—it stretches over 843 acres (about 3.4 million square meters)! It's a great place to play and enjoy some green space right in the middle of the big city. Central Park was the first public park in America—and it is the most popular city park in the nation 😮. Have you seen Central Park in the movies? Many, many movies have had scenes set in Central Park. The park was designed by Frederick Law Olmsted and Calvert Vaux.

Must-Dos:

☐ Take a stroll and look at all the statues of famous people from history. Do you recognize any from your studies in school?

_____

☐ Climb aboard the Central Park Carousel and spin around on one of the largest carousels in the United States. It is over 100 years old! Plus, all of its horses are hand carved!

☐ Visit the Swedish Cottage Marionette Theatre. It puts on a variety of plays during the summer and school year.

 What was your favorite memory from Central Park?

_____

Tip! If you visit during wintertime, make sure to go to the ice rink in Central Park. If you go at night, you can skate under the stars and the lights from the city.

Did you know?

Central Park was under construction before the American Civil War started. They got permission to build on that land in 1853, and they kept building it throughout the war, until it was completed in 1873.

Central Park Zoo—see 1,400+ animals

More than 1,400 animals live at the Central Park Zoo and Wildlife Center! Leonardo says that it's a wonderful place to spend the day with your family. You can visit the main zoo, or feed the animals at the Tisch Children's Zoo—where you can hop and climb and pretend to be an animal!

The zoo was added after the park was built. In 1864, it became only the second publicly owned zoo in America.

Which animals were your favorites to watch?

_____

_____

_____

_____

Did you know?

A newspaper called the *New York Herald* once wrote a story claiming that animals had escaped from the zoo and were running around the city. Luckily, the story was a hoax (they made it up)!

The one and only Times Square!

Times Square is a dazzling display of lights and buildings in the heart of Manhattan. It's known for its bright and moving advertisements. Times Square is often called the Crossroads of the World or the Center of the Universe. It is one of the most visited places in the world, seen by millions and millions of tourists a year 😊.

Square to Square
Times Square was originally called Longacre Square. It was renamed in 1904 after the Times Building was built.

Take a Walk
In 2009, the mayor of NYC declared Times Square to be a pedestrian-only place. Now, no cars are allowed to drive through Times Square.

Happy New Year!
The dropping of the shining crystal ball on New Year's Eve is a tradition that started in 1907.

Let There Be Light
The first electric advertisement was lit in 1904.

Bad Reputation
Before electric streetlights, the Times Square area was dark and dangerous. It was known as Thieves Lair, because of all its pickpockets and thieves.

There are many costumed characters wandering around Times Square. Which characters did you see?

_____

_____

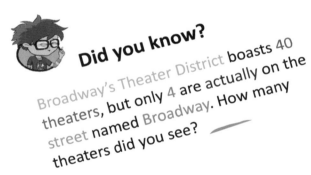

Give your regards to Broadway!

Broadway Street is one of the oldest roads in Manhattan. It goes back to the days when New York was called New Amsterdam. Since then, it has become known worldwide as the Theater District. It's also sometimes called the Great White Way. Broadway's live performances are always happening. Some famous shows run for many years.

Did you know?

If a Broadway show is popular enough, it could run for many years. Andrew Lloyd Weber's *Phantom of the Opera* is the longest-running play of all time. It's been on Broadway for over 25 years, with over 10,000 performances.

Did you know?

Broadway's Theater District boasts 40 theaters, but only 4 are actually on the street named Broadway. How many theaters did you see?

Look at the posters and advertisements as you travel down Broadway. Can you unscramble these names of famous plays?

EHT IONL GINK _____

TCAS _____

DEWIKC _____

YBEUAT DAN HTE SETAB _____

NEIAN _____

YM RAIF LDYA _____

Wonders of the Met—Metropolitan Museum of Art

Called the Met for short, this is the largest art museum in the United States—and one of the biggest in the world 😮. It is home to many paintings, sculptures, musical instruments, antique weapons, historic clothing, and many other things from all sorts of time periods!

Which Came First?

Using the boxes, can you number each time period so that they are in order from earliest to most recent?

Medieval

Egyptian

Modern

Greco-Roman

Famous artists at the Met

The **Metropolitan Museum of Art** first opened in 1872. It was planned as a place for people to learn about art and culture. Today, admission to the **Met** is free—but you can pay something if you want to donate to the museum.

Try to find artists' names that begin with each letter as you walk around the museum. Leonardo has already filled some in for you!

A _____

B _____

C _____

D _____

E _Édouard Manet_

F _____

G _____

H _____

I _____

J _____

K _____

L _____

M _____

N _____

O _____

P _____

Q _____

R _____

S _____

T _____

U _____

V _____

W _____

X _____

Y _Yang Xu_

Z _Zumpe Johannes_

Tip! Be sure to use the artist's first and last name.

Did you know?

The Met has almost two million square feet (about 186,000 square meters) of space. That's as big as 35 American football fields—or 26 soccer fields !

21

The Brooklyn Bridge— walk or drive across

You probably have been driving around a bit by now, and you may have either seen or driven on the Brooklyn Bridge. The bridge crosses the East River. It was built in 1883, and it's one of the oldest suspension bridges in the United States.

Did you know?

When this bridge was built, it was the longest suspension bridge in the world. There were many problems while building it, but they finally succeeded and gave us a great landmark to admire.

Did you cross the bridge by walking or driving?

Walk / Drive

When you crossed the bridge, how long did it take you?

_____

Family Business

The Brooklyn Bridge was designed by John Roebling. His son, Washington, took over building it after his father got sick. But Washington got sick, too, with caisson disease. That's a disease that comes from diving deep down into water and then coming back up too fast. This causes gases in the body to bubble, like when you blow into a glass of milk. Washington's wife, Emily, learned advanced math to help him with the bridge project. She was the first person to walk across the bridge after it was completed.

Coney Island—exciting rides and more ...

Coney Island is known for its amusement parks and resort-like atmosphere. Tourists have been going there for almost 200 years ☺! People started visiting the area as a vacation spot as early as the 1830s.

Did you go on any amusement rides? Which ones?

_____

_____

Coney Island isn't actually an island—it's a peninsula. A peninsula is attached to land on one end, but the other three sides stretch out into the water. The picture below shows how Coney Island looks from an airplane.

 **Tip!** Visit the New York Aquarium and take a stroll down the boardwalk.

Leonardo likes Coney Island very much!

What do you think about Coney Island?

Ask your family too ...

I like it very much _____

Don't like it _____

Did you know?

"Coney" comes from the Dutch word *conyne*, which means rabbit. Instead of saying "bunny," they used to say "coney"!

Empire State Building— world-famous Views

LEONARDO'S TIP: The Empire State Building is a place you must see when you visit **NYC**. It's one of the most famous buildings in the world 😮! The Empire State Building represents the strength of America and New York City.

FAST FACTS

The Empire State Building was completed in 1931. How many years ago was that? _____

It was the tallest building in the world for almost 40 years, until the World Trade Center was completed in 1970.

The building's grand opening happened during the Great Depression. Because times were so bad, the Empire State Building had hardly any tenants until the 1950s.

It has become a symbol in pop culture, appearing in many movies and TV shows.

Have you seen the Empire State Building in any shows that you enjoy?

_____

_____

_____

Quizzes! How many stories does the Empire State Building have?

1. 55
2. 82
3. 103
4. 150

ANSWER: 3. 103

Exploring Rockefeller Center

Have you heard of the Rockefellers? They were very rich. John D. Rockefeller was a businessman who was America's first billionaire. His son, John D. Rockefeller Jr., built Rockefeller Center. It's the home of several businesses, and it has a waterfall, several statues, and even a popular skating rink in wintertime.

Radio City Music Hall in Rockefeller Center is the world's largest indoor theater—and its marquee stretches a whole city block. Top entertainers perform there, including rock and pop stars.

Since the theater opened in 1932, the *Radio City Christmas Spectacular* has been a family favorite. It stars the women's dance team "The Rockettes." The popular "Parade of the Wooden Soldiers" and "Living Nativity" have been part of the show for over 80 years.

Would you like to be a Rockette?

Women have to be at least 18 and between 5' 6" and 5' 10-1/2" (between about 1.68 and 1.8 meters) tall, and be very good dancers! The Rockettes do "precision" dance—a mixture of ballet, jazz, tap, and modern dance.

Rockefeller designed his center to be full of art and beauty. Here are pictures of a couple of the most famous statues there.

Find the statues!

Leonardo loves the statues in Rockefeller Center, but he can't find their names. Can you help him?

The golden statue in the photo below is _____. He is a character from Greek mythology who stole fire from the gods and gave knowledge to humans.

This statue above is another character from Greek mythology. _____ lost in a war against the gods. He was forced to carry the weight of the world on his shoulders forever as a punishment.

Ellis Island—"Gateway to America"

America is a country of immigrants. And Ellis Island was America's busiest immigration station from 1892 until 1954. Over 12 million immigrants arrived there during that time. Today Ellis Island is an immigration museum.

of old

nowadays

Tip! Stand in the middle of the great room and imagine it full of people all speaking different languages—but all trying to find a better life in America.

Did you know?

In the beginning, Ellis Island was a very small island. But they took the dirt removed from digging New York City's subway tunnels and added it to the island—making the island twice as big!

Photo Opportunity

Outside of the Registry Room is the Kissing Post. This is where families, friends, and spouses would meet and greet each other after arriving on Ellis Island. This is a great place to take a photo with your own family!

PASTE A PICTURE OF YOUR FAMILY.

Ellis Island—why some were turned away

Not everyone who came to America got the dream they hoped for. Many families were split up when some members weren't allowed to enter the country.

In order to be processed, the travelers would have to answer some questions. They would need to prove that they could work to support themselves and also that they were not sick. People with diseases or criminal records would be sent back to the country they came from—while those with good health and job possibilities would be allowed to enter the United States.

 My favorite Ellis Island story:

_____

_____

_____

_____

Statue of Liberty ...
lifting the lamp of freedom

Have you heard about the Statue of Liberty? Well, Leonardo will tell you all about it ...

This huge statue was a gift from France to the United States on America's 100th birthday. It was meant to celebrate France's friendship with America—and the importance of freedom and independence. It's also called Lady Liberty. The statue is based on Libertas, the Roman goddess of liberty. It was designed by Frenchman Frederic-Auguste Bartholdi.

 The statue was dedicated in

_____

Lady Liberty stands tall on Liberty Island, near Ellis Island. Immigrants traveling to Ellis Island by boat would have sailed right past the statue as they came to America.

There is a poem printed on a plaque at the base of the statue, written by Emma Lazarus. Can you remember its most famous line?

_____

Did you know?

The statue was hammered out of sheets of copper. Copper is a bronze color, but as the statue has been exposed to the air and seawater, it has slowly turned from copper to its current green color.

ANSWERS

It was dedicated in 1886.
The poem's most famous line:
"Give me your tired, your poor, your huddled masses yearning to breathe free."

Statue of Liberty

Quizzes!

1. How many rays shine from Liberty's crown?

A. 6
B. 10
C. 7
D. 8

2. Where was the Statue of Liberty made?

A. Washington, DC
B. Berlin, Germany
C. Paris, France
D. New York City

3. Who wrote the poem that is engraved on the base of the statue?

A. Emma Lazarus
B. Michael Jackson
C. George W. Bush
D. George Washington

4. What is Liberty standing on (other than the pedestal)?

A. Water
B. The world
C. People
D. Chains

5. From which metal is the shell of the statue made?

A. Iron
B. Copper
C. Gold
D. Platinum

ANSWERS

1-C, 2-C, 3-A, 4-D, 5-B

9/11 Memorial ...
honoring the Victims

The **9/11 Memorial** was created at the spot where the **World Trade Center** towers were destroyed.

Leonardo will tell you how it happened ...

In 2001, two planes were hijacked and flown into the buildings, killing nearly 3,000 people. It was a very sad day ... 😠. This site is now called Ground Zero. Two reflection ponds cover the holes left in the ground where each tower used to stand. You can see one of them in the photo below. The pool is surrounded by the names of everyone who died in the tragic event.

Besides the **Twin Towers**, the Pentagon was also struck by a third plane, causing damage to the building and taking more lives.

Did you know?

Washington, DC, was also supposed to be part of the attack. But some brave passengers on the plane headed there fought the hijackers, saving many lives.

At night, these pillars of light shine up into the sky where the towers used to stand.

American Museum of Natural History— so much to see!

Across the street from Central Park, you'll find one of the largest and most popular museums in the world. *The museum is huge!* It covers 1.6 million square feet (146,000 square meters)—or the size of 28 American football fields 😮.

The American Museum of Natural History was founded in 1869. It was originally built right in Central Park. But its collection got so big, it had to be moved to its much larger current space.

Museum Summary

Favorite exhibit: _____
_____

Most interesting exhibit: _____
_____

Most boring exhibit: _____
_____

An interesting fact I learned: _____
_____

Did you know?

In 1991, the museum installed a mold of a dinosaur called Barosaurus that is five stories high—the tallest in the world!

Museum of Natural History— Looking from outer space

Earth looks very different from space! Can you use the word bank and figure out what each picture below shows?

Word Bank

Great Wall of China   New York City

Iceland   Grand Canyon

This is a natural formation in Arizona.
It's in a national park with the same name.

This country has the smallest population of any nation in Europe.

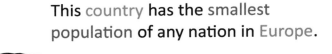

This city is often referred to as the capital of the world.

This man-made structure was built as a shield against invaders.

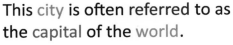

It's all happening at Madison Square Garden!

Sporting events like hockey and basketball, big parties, music concerts, horse shows, and more all happen at Madison Square Garden. It is one of the largest multipurpose stadiums in the world. New Yorkers just call it "The Garden." Can you imagine all the work it takes to transform it from a hockey ice rink to a horse show arena ?

Look at the billboard and the banners outside of Madison Square Garden. Which events are coming soon to The Garden? Try to figure out whether each event is a sporting event, a party, or a concert.

Concerts: _____

_____

Sporting Events: _____

_____

Parties: _____

_____

Did you know?

Performers dream of "selling out" Madison Square Garden. Many have done exactly that, but no one has done it as quickly as Taylor Swift. In 2009 she sold every ticket to her Madison Square Garden **concert** in 60 seconds (only one minute) !

Did you know?

The first artificial ice-skating rink in the United States opened at Madison Square Garden in 1879.

Yankee Stadium—play ball!

Yankee Stadium is home to the New York Yankees, a Major League Baseball team. This new ballpark opened in 2009, but it honors the old one by keeping some of its famous history.

☐ Visit the New York Yankees Museum in the ballpark to learn more about their history.

☐ Take a guided tour of the stadium.

My favorite part of Yankee Stadium:

_____

_____

An interesting fact I learned:

_____

_____

Did you know?

There is a group of people who call themselves the Bleacher Creatures. They say they are the "real" fans of the Yankees! They all sit in a certain section of the stadium to cheer the team.

The great New York Yankees!

The Yankees are one of the most successful teams in the history of baseball. The team was founded in 1903, but they didn't take the name "Yankees" until 1913. That means they have been around for over 100 years!

Each baseball team has a different uniform.

What are the official colors of the Yankees uniforms?

A. Red and blue with white stars

B. Navy-blue, white, and gray

C. Navy-blue, green, and yellow

Leonardo wants to start a new baseball team. Help him design his new team's uniform by coloring the picture.

New York Yankees team logo

ANSWER
B. Navy-blue, white, and gray

BRONX ZOO

Bronx Zoo—6,000 animals and counting

The Bronx Zoo is one of the largest city zoos in the world! It has over 6,000 animals. The zoo was built so that the Bronx River flows right through it. It first opened in 1899.

If your feet get tired of walking around the zoo, hail a horse-drawn carriage and ride around the zoo in style.

You've now seen a couple of zoos since you started your trip in NYC. How would you rank them?

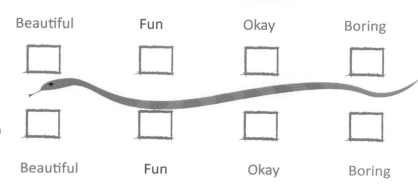

	Beautiful	Fun	Okay	Boring
Bronx Zoo	☐	☐	☐	☐
Central Park Zoo	☐	☐	☐	☐
	Beautiful	Fun	Okay	Boring

Tip!

You can bring in your own food and have a picnic on the grounds. What a fun way to spend the afternoon!

Which zoo was your favorite?

_____

Why? _____

Did you notice a river flowing through many of the animal habitats? That's the Bronx River, and the zoo was built around it.

Visit summary

How long did we stay in New York City? _____

At which hotel did we stay? _____

What kinds of transportation did we use? _____

Which places did we visit? _____
_____
_____

The souvenirs I bought in New York City are: _____

The best food I ate in New York City was: _____

Record each family member's favorite places:

_____ : _____
_____ : _____
_____ : _____
_____ : _____

My favorite place in New York City is: _____

New York City games!

Quizzes!

Who am I?

Can you guess which New York City site is being described?

1. I am known for "America's Pastime," but I attract thousands of people at a time for sports, music, and more. I was built recently, so I am shiny and new for people to come and have a good time.

_____

2. Millions of people came to me, looking for a new start.

_____

3. People come to me from all over to see performances that they have always loved or to find new ones to love.

_____

TRIVIA!

1. Which New York City site includes the saying "Never forget"?

   a. Central Park Zoo   b. 9/11 Memorial   c. Ellis Island

2. How many stories tall is the Empire State Building?

   a. 103   b. 42   c. 7

3. Before it was called New York City, what was the city's official name?

   a. New Hamsterdam   b. Old York   c. New Amsterdam

ANSWERS

Trivia: 1. b, 2. a, 3. c

Who Am I? 1. Yankee Stadium, 2. Ellis Island, 3. Broadway

Can you break the code?

Use the key below to decode Leonardo's journal entry about his trip to New York City!

H = U   Z = O   X = E   J = I

I had a great time in NXW YZRK CJTY (_ _ _ _ _ _ _ _ _ _ _)! I saw a lot of cool animals, explored a few museums, and got to play on a BXACh (_ _ _ _ _)!

One of my favorite places to visit was the Museum of Natural History, where I learned about all kinds of things like rocks, fossils, and DJNZSAHRS (_ _ _ _ _ _ _ _ _). There sure are a lot of interesting animals in the world! At YANKXX STADJHM (_ _ _ _ _ _ _ _ _ _ _ _ _), we saw lots of interesting people, and I got to watch a baseball game!

But my favorite part about New York City was ThX STATHX ZF LJBXRTY (_ _ _ _ _ _ _ _ _ _ _ _ _ _ _ _). Then again, I also loved walking around TJMXS SQHARX (_ _ _ _ _ _ _ _ _ _) and seeing some plays on BRZADWAY (_ _ _ _ _ _ _ _). I guess I loved XVXRYThJNG (_ _ _ _ _ _ _ _ _ _) about wonderful New York City!

Connect the Names of These Famous NYC Sites

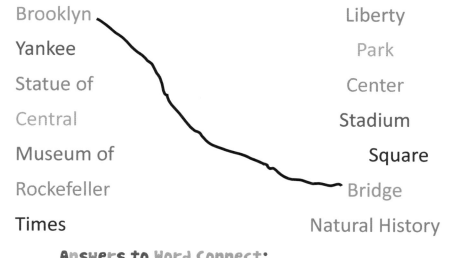

Brooklyn	Liberty
Yankee	Park
Statue of	Center
Central	Stadium
Museum of	Square
Rockefeller	Bridge
Times	Natural History

Answers to Word Connect:

Brooklyn Bridge, Yankee Stadium, Statue of Liberty, Central Park, Museum of Natural History, Rockefeller Center, Times Square

My NYC journal

Date

What did we do?

_____   _____
_____   _____
_____   _____
_____   _____
_____   _____
_____   _____
_____   _____
_____   _____
_____   _____
_____   _____
_____   _____

Acknowledgment: All images are from Shutterstock or public domain except those mentioned below:
Attribution: 15mt1-Dylan's Candy Bar, New York City By Casper Moller [Attribution 2.0 Generic (CC BY 2.0)]; 15mt2 This photo was taken by participant/team NewYorkDolls as part of the Commons:Wikipedia Takes Manhattan project on April 4, 2008; 15mc-By Jim.Henderson (Own work) [CC0], via Wikimedia Commons; 15mb1-By Marcin Wichary from San Francisco, U.S.A. (Entertainers Uploaded by Neukoln) [CC BY 2.0 (http://creativecommons.org/licenses/by/2.0), via Wikimedia Commons; 17mc-By stignygaard (Flickr) [CC BY 2.0 (http://creativecommons.org/licenses/by/2.0)], via Wikimedia Commons; 20m- Codrin.B / Wikimedia Commons; via Wikimedia Commons 31mt2-By Anagoria (Own work) [GFDL (http://www.gnu.org/copyleft/fdl.html) or CC BY 3.0 (http://creativecommons.org/licenses/by/3.0)], via Wikimedia Commons; 31mbr-By Greg from New York, NY, America (Christina fights the dragon) [CC BY 2.0 (http://creativecommons.org/licenses/by/2.0) via Wikimedia Commons; 31mt-By Gigi Alt (Own work) [CC BY-SA 3.0 (http://creativecommons.org/licenses/by-sa/3.0)], via Wikimedia Commons; 33bg-By Andrés Nieto Porras from Palma de Mallorca, España (Madison Square Garden Uploaded by russavia) [CC BY-SA 2.0 (http://creativecommons.org/licenses/by-sa/2.0)], via Wikimedia Commons; 33mb-By Jana Zills Uploaded by MyCanon (Taylor Swift) [CC BY 2.0 (http://creativecommons.org/licenses/by/2.0)], via Wikimedia Commons; 33mc-By Nyr3188 at en.wikipedia [public domain], from Wikimedia Commons; 34bg-Silent Wind of Doom at the English language Wikipedia [CC BY 3.0 (http://creativecommons.org/licenses/by/3.0)], via Wikimedia Commons; 34m-By Beyond My Ken (Own work) [GFDL (http://www.gnu.org/copyleft/fdl.html) or CC BY-SA 4.0-3.0-2.5-2.0-1.0 (http://creativecommons.org/licenses/by-sa/4.0-3...)], via Wikimedia Commons; 35bg-Madisonsquaregarden by Baschti84; 36bg-By Colin (originally posted to Flickr as bronx zoo) [CC BY-SA 2.0 (http://creativecommons.org/licenses/by-sa/2.0)], via Wikimedia Commons.

Key: t=top;
b=bottom;
l=left;
r=right;
c=center;
m=main image;
bg=background

Printed in Great Britain
by Amazon